THE

Feng Shui JOURNAL

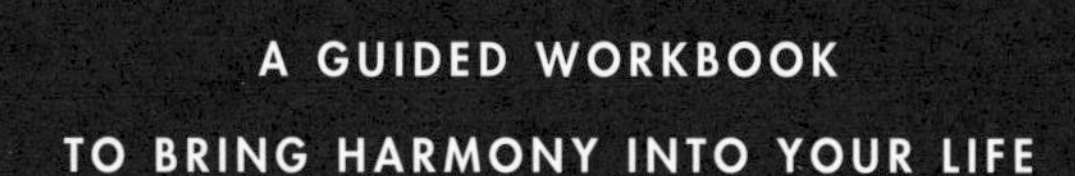

A GUIDED WORKBOOK
TO BRING HARMONY INTO YOUR LIFE

BY TERESA POLANCO
Illustrated by Chris Paschke

PETER PAUPER PRESS, INC.
WHITE PLAINS, NEW YORK

CONTENTS

INTRODUCTION

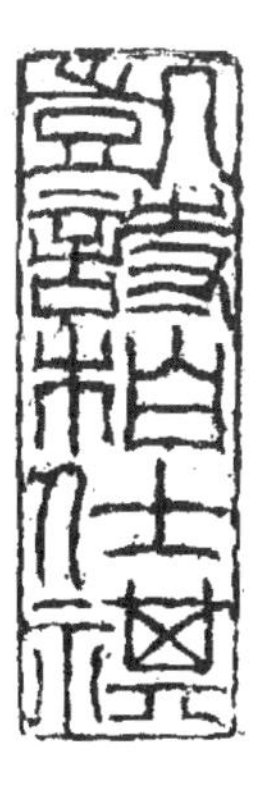

FENG SHUI (PRONOUNCED *FUNG SHWAY*) IS A CHINESE DISCIPLINE that seeks to establish harmony and balance in our lives and our environment. It reveals how our living space—home, garden, office—mirrors our lives. By harnessing the positive aspects of nature, we can create vital new energy for ourselves. When this energy begins to permeate all areas of our life—family, career, health, creativity—we can begin to thrive and prosper.

When we design our space with purpose, we experience a heightened field of energy. As we begin to live more mindfully, we feel better and perform better. When we ignore an area of our environment, we are subconsciously ignoring a specific area of our life. This usually means there are underlying issues that we do not yet recognize or prefer not to address. Feng shui allows us to get to the core issues faster and change the way we live permanently, from within.

THE *BAGUA*

TO ANALYZE OUR ENVIRONMENT, we use an eight-sided map called the *bagua*, which divides our life into nine major areas. The bagua shows us where the different life areas fall in our individual space, whether home or office. The bagua areas can be applied to different parts of our space, from our yard, home, or office, to each separate floor, each room, and even a bed or desk.

The bagua is read from the bottom up, as if we are standing at the door of a house looking in. The front door of the space is the main mouth of *chi*, or energy.

Looking at the bagua—that is, looking into our space—we see:

- at the far left, the area of prosperity;
- at the far right, the area of relationships;
- at the far center, the area of fame and recognition—how we see ourselves;
- on the center right, the area of creativity, children, and potential;
- on the center left, the area of family, ancestors, and new beginnings;
- at the absolute center of the home, the area of overall health.

A door can be positioned in one of three places on the entrance wall:

- to the right of center, the area of helpful people, mentors, and travel;
- at the center, the area of your career or journey in life;
- to the left of center, the area of knowledge, self-cultivation, studies, and spiritual development.

PROSPERITY #4 Wood Hipbone Southeast Eldest daughter purple, green, red	FAME #9 Fire Eyes South Middle daughter red, green, pink	RELATIONSHIPS #2 Earth Abdomen Southwest Mother pink, yellow, red, white
FAMILY/GROWTH #3 Wood Foot East Eldest son green, blue, purple	HEALTH #5 Earth All other body parts Center 7th child yellow, orange, gold, clay	CREATIVITY/ CHILDREN #7 Metal Mouth West Youngest daughter white, pastels
KNOWLEDGE #8 Earth Hand Northeast Youngest son blue, green	CAREER #1 Water Ears North Middle son black, blue, green	HELPFUL PEOPLE/TRAVEL #6 Metal Head Northwest Father gray, black, silver

Entrance

USING THE JOURNAL

THIS JOURNAL IS DIVIDED INTO TEN SECTIONS—a general introduction, plus one section for each of the nine life areas of the bagua. At the beginning of each section, you'll find the qualities and characteristics associated with that life area—number, natural element, direction, colors—all of which can be integrated into your space. Next follow Revealing Exercises to help you evaluate the feng shui of the area. The Applications part of each section describes actions you can take to improve feng shui. The journal leaves plenty of space for recording feelings, changes, and progress in each area of your life. Good luck with your feng shui journey, and may the *chi* be with you!

Revealing Exercises

1. Before you can begin to use feng shui effectively, you must clarify your intentions. Are you ready to proceed with deliberation and apply yourself with purpose? Take time to write out in specific detail the changes you would like to make. You need to see yourself living the new changes—see them, feel them, smell them, taste them. Be sure to include specific things you do *not* want to do, as well. Write this statement of intention and commitment on the following pages of the journal. Keep the journal handy, in a special place.

2. Carefully draw the floor plan of your entire space, floor-by-floor, on the following pages. Label the front door and each of the rooms. Mark doors, windows, and major pieces of furniture. Note the overall shape of the floor plan. Is it U-shaped? Is it shaped like a boot? Ideally, you want to work with a complete square or rectangle. If your space has an irregular shape, complete any missing areas of the rectangle with a dotted line. Consult the examples below for guidance. You will refer to your floor plan for various exercises.

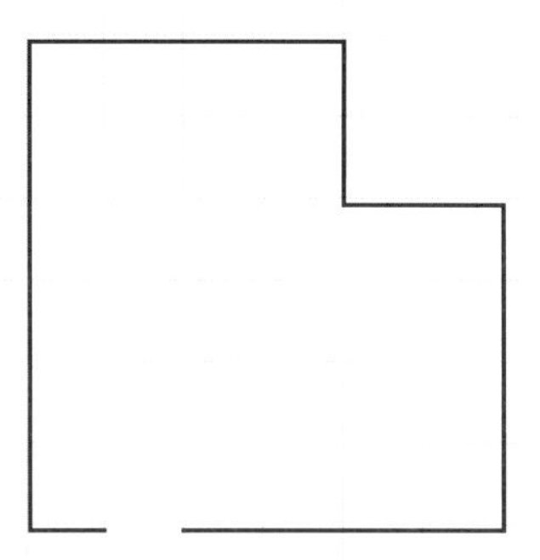

SAMPLE FLOOR PLAN
WITH MISSING
RELATIONSHIP CORNER

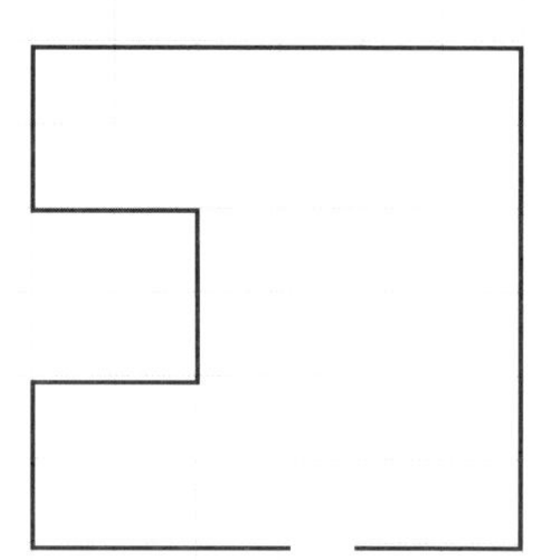

SAMPLE FLOOR PLAN
WITH MISSING
FAMILY AREA

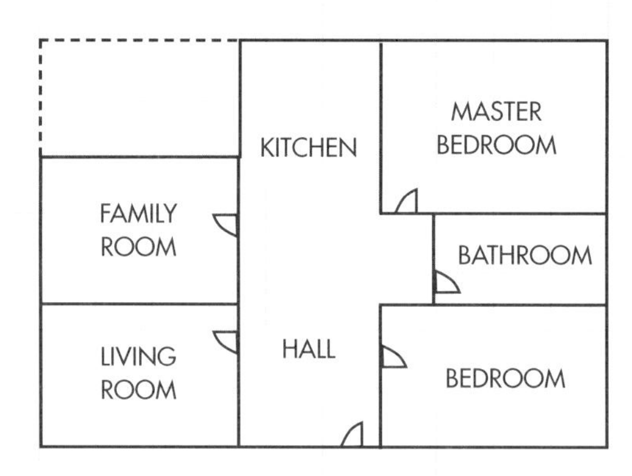

SAMPLE FLOOR PLAN
WITH DOTTED LINE TO
COMPLETE MISSING CORNER

3. Take a moment to consider that all objects in your space trigger feelings, both positive and negative. What is the first thing you see upon waking, and how does it make you feel?

4. What is the last thing you see before leaving your home in the morning? Does it help start your day well?

5. What is the first thing that you see upon returning home? Does it calm you down or rev you up?

6. After a hectic day, what is the last thing you see before closing your eyes? How does it make you feel?

IDEALLY, everything in your space should be sacred to you. You should love and feel inspired by each part of your surroundings. Only then can the exchange of positive and harmonious energy take place. The exercises in this journal will show you how to achieve this goal.

Applications

1. Clutter causes energy to stagnate. It is more difficult to access prosperous energy when stacks of old magazines and boxes of trinkets fill your prosperity corner. Keep in mind that objects and patterns of behavior that no longer serve you prevent new, fortunate blessings from entering your life. Get rid of these things. Give them to others who are truly in need, so that you can begin to accumulate positive energy and discover new opportunities.

Exercise:

Think about areas you need to clean up. What would you like to do with the extra energy you gain from creating order in your life? Complete the following sentences to match your personal needs.

Example: My intention **this week** is to clean out the bedroom closet in my prosperity corner so that I may accomplish the following: a 10% increase in my monthly income by securing one new business contact, so that I am able to pay off my car loan within 6 months.

- My intention **this week** is to clean out the ________________ in my ________________ corner so that I may accomplish the following: ________________

• My intention **next week** is to clean out the ______

in my ______ corner so that I may accomplish the following: ______

• My intention in **a month** is to have cleaned out the ______

in my ______ corner so that I may accomplish the following: ______

• My intention in **six months** is to have cleaned out the ______

in my ______ corner so that I may accomplish the following: ______

• My intention in **a year** is to have cleaned out the ______

in my ______ corner so that I may accomplish the following: ______

2. Take before and after photographs of the specific areas of your home in which you intend to manifest changes—your prosperity corner, for example. Tape or paste the photos on the pages that follow. In each of the nine life areas in the journal, you can keep a record of the feng shui changes as you make them.

With powerful and pure intention, it is likely that you will see progress between a new moon and a full moon. Auspicious times to implement feng shui design changes are between 11:00 a.m. and 1:00 p.m., or 11:00 p.m. and 1:00 a.m., as you can tap into the increased energies of the sun and moon at these times.

ALL LIFE IS VIBRATION. YOU COMBINE WITH WHAT YOU NOTICE, OR YOU COMBINE WITH WHAT YOU VIBRATE TO. IF YOU ARE VIBRATING TO INJUSTICE AND RESENTMENT YOU WILL MEET IT ON YOUR PATHWAY, AT EVERY STEP.

FLORENCE SCOVEL SHINN

THE ART OF LIFE
LIES IN A CONSTANT
READJUSTMENT TO OUR
SURROUNDINGS.

OKAKURA KAKUZO

木墨
設計

3. To begin your day feeling energized, place stimulating, active, and uplifting pictures—rainbows, waterfalls, sunrises—in the areas you see upon waking and upon leaving your home.

4. To end your day in a peaceful mood, place calming and soothing pictures—gently drifting sailboats, a softly fading sunset—in the entry area of your home and near your bed.

• ~ •

Notes:

WE SHAPE OUR BUILDINGS; THEREAFTER THEY SHAPE US.

WINSTON CHURCHILL

A HOME IS NOT DEAD BUT LIVING, AND LIKE ALL LIVING THINGS MUST OBEY THE LAWS OF NATURE BY CONSTANTLY CHANGING.

CARL LARSSON

RELATIONSHIPS

THIS AREA OF THE BAGUA corresponds to our relationships with others and our ability to receive. Our receptiveness is compared to that of the earth, patiently receiving the farmer's seed. Relationships can be with spouse, lover, children, families, community, career, or ourselves. Here we will consider the relationship with the "significant other."

ELEMENT: earth—the receptive, the receiver
CHARACTERISTICS: firm but not rigid; stable, reliable; still but not stagnant
COLORS: pink, yellow, red, white
SHAPE: low, flat, square; plateau
NUMBER: two
DIRECTION: southwest
BODY PART: abdomen
FAMILY MEMBER: mother
AREA: to the far right, when standing at the door looking inward

REVEALING EXERCISES

1. Stand at the door to your bedroom. List the objects you have placed in your relationship area, at the far right corner of the room.

TVs or computers in this area suggest voids or deficiencies in the relationship; the focus tends to be on things rather than on the partner. These objects also create electromagnetic radiation, which drains energy from the body. The bedroom is a special, sacred place and should be considered with respect if the relationship is to blossom.

2. Refer to your floor plan. Note whether the relationship area is missing from the overall shape of the plan. Missing relationship areas may cause a woman to feel unsettled in her home or impact her sense of femininity, as this area is directly associated with female, or yin, energy. In this case, it may be more challenging to attract and sustain relationship energy in general. The applications on page 30 suggest several ways to remedy this deficiency.

3. Take notice of the objects in the far right area of other parts of your environment. List the things you have placed in the relationship corner:

- in the living room:

- in the kitchen:

- in the office:

4. Moving through your entire space, list the items that are representative of your relationship. Note exactly where these items are located.

Applications

1. To harness missing relationship energy, work to integrate the relationship colors, number, element, and other symbols into your space. Discover relationship symbols with special meaning for you—a painting of a loving couple, a pear tree ripe with Earth's abundance, a beautiful plant in full bloom. Display your marriage certificate, toasting glasses, wedding presents, and cake figurine alongside gifts from your partner.

2. Remove from relationship areas all objects representing singleness—for example, a single photo of a woman reading, a male statue, a candle in a holder, a chair. Replace these single objects with pairs.

3. Place photos of you and your significant other in the relationship areas of your space. A solid relationship is the key to a strong, loving family. Photos of children may be better placed in the family or children areas. Ensure that photos and portraits in the relationship areas are updated from time to time, bringing vital energy to the space and sustenance to the relationship.

4. Equality in a relationship helps create harmony in our lives. Make sure that night tables in the bedroom are of equal size and shape, and that there is an equal amount of space on each side of the bed. Neither person should have greater access or freedom of movement.

5. In this area, place books, CDs, and tapes that encourage growth and renewal. Avoid negative material on relationships here, such as books on communication difficulties between partners.

6. Make sure that whatever pieces you hang on your walls are balanced. Off-center objects could throw your relationship off course.

7. The two-piece box spring of a king-size bed divides energy in a relationship. Join the two box springs by placing a king-size sheet over them; or, place a piece of red fabric over the division to unify the energy.

8. Create a treasure chest of love that holds your fondest memories. Incorporate things you have made together, activities you have done as a couple, objects representing the loving bond that unites you. Place in the box copies of your favorite songs, poems, books, cards, and treasures, including words with special meaning, secret gestures, "pet" names. Every few months, plan to celebrate your love. Open the chest, update it, and share it with others. Renew the energy in the chest and the energy that keeps you together.

9. Use the Relationship Journal. Communicate to each other the delights and frustrations of your love. Be open and honest. Honor your union by nurturing it.

THE FRAGRANCE
ALWAYS STAYS IN
THE HAND THAT GIVES
THE ROSE.

HADA BEJAR

WE CAN ONLY LEARN TO LOVE BY LOVING.

DORIS MURDOCK

NOBODY HAS EVER MEASURED, EVEN POETS, HOW MUCH THE HEART CAN HOLD.

ZELDA FITZGERALD

MARRIAGE IS THE HIGHEST MYSTERY.

NOVALIS

For the mature person, the Tao begins in the relationship between man and woman, and ends in the infinite vastness of the universe.

Tzu-ssu

水墨
設計

SELF-UNDERSTANDING IS ONE OF THE MAIN PURPOSES OF PHILOSOPHY—TO UNDERSTAND THE RELATIONSHIPS OF MEN, THINGS, AND WORDS TO EACH OTHER.

ISAIAH BERLIN

CAREER

THIS AREA OF OUR LIFE REPRESENTS our journey, career, and passions—the reality of doing what we want to be doing.

ELEMENT: water
CHARACTERISTICS: fluidity, reflection, deepness, stillness;
liquid requiring containment
COLORS: black, blue, and green
SHAPES: irregular, wavy
NUMBER: one
DIRECTION: north
BODY PART: ears
FAMILY MEMBER: middle son
AREA: around the center of the entrance wall. The door may be placed in this area.

Revealing Exercises

Check the most appropriate response. If none applies, fill in the blank with the word of your choice.

1. Upon entering my workspace, I feel:

❑ relieved ❑ happy ❑ anxious ❑ annoyed ❑ other

____

____

2. Upon entering my workspace, I smell:

❑ nothing ❑ chemicals ❑ sweet fragrances ❑ food ❑ other

____

____

3. The door to my home or office:

❑ opens easily ❑ needs to be forced open ❑ rubs against the flooring or doorframe ❑ other

____

____

4. Upon entering my home or office, I face:

❑ a wall ❑ an open space ❑ a staircase ❑ a column ❑ other

____

____

APPLICATIONS

1. If the door to your home or office is within the career area, ensure that it opens easily and freely. It should not stick, jam, or rub against anything. If it does, you may feel stuck in your career. To avoid constant obstacles on the job, make sure there are no obstructions in your physical pathway.

2. Make a conscious effort to use the front door to both home and office, even if another door is more convenient. Not using the front door is equivalent to ignoring whatever aspect of your life the door falls within—usually career, knowledge, or helpful people. Energy begins to stagnate. New energy cannot enter freely and career opportunities will be harder to find.

3. The three possible placements of the front door hold different meanings for your career. The door in the center represents how you are known. The door to the left of center represents what you know, and the door to the right of center represents whom you know.

4. The placement of items on the inside of the wall holding the door represents the different stages of your life. This holds true for both home and office. The top part of the wall represents the future, the bottom part refers to the past, and the center signifies the present. You can activate these areas according to your needs and intentions.

5. In order to get things moving in your career, try introducing water. Set up a water fountain that flows into your career space or hang a picture of water there. Recreate rapid movement if you want quick, strong results, or a more constant, flowing movement if you desire continuity. Install a fish tank with live fish that keep the water constantly moving.

6. If you face a column when entering the career area of your home, you may be given choices of what direction to take or which career path to follow. Place an area rug along the path you prefer. If your career requires abstract, creative thinking, create a stronger path to the right. If your work requires more concrete, logical thinking, define a stronger path to the left.

7. If you face a wall when entering the career area of your office or home, put up a mirror to draw the energy further into the space, giving the illusion that the wall has disappeared. Or, hang a picture that draws you into it. Both will alleviate career roadblocks.

IF YOU HEAR A VOICE WITHIN YOU SAYING, "YOU ARE NOT A PAINTER," THEN BY ALL MEANS PAINT . . . AND THAT VOICE WILL BE SILENCED.

VINCENT VAN GOGH

DO NOT FEAR GOING FORWARD SLOWLY; FEAR ONLY STANDING STILL.

CHINESE PROVERB

GOALS ARE DREAMS WITH DEADLINES.

DIANA SCHARF HUNT

木墨
設計

THE FACT THAT OUR TASK IS EXACTLY AS LARGE AS OUR LIFE MAKES IT APPEAR INFINITE.

FRANZ KAFKA

水墨
設計

When you work you are a flute through whose heart the whispering of the hours turns to music. To love life through labor is to be intimate with life's inmost secret. All work is empty save when there is love, for work is love made visible.

Kahlil Gibran

PROSPERITY

THIS AREA REPRESENTS the fortunate blessings in life, from health and children to financial prosperity.

ELEMENT: wood
CHARACTERISTICS: expansive, upward movement; consuming, creating, sprouting
COLORS: green, purple, red
SHAPE: tall, thin, pillar-like
NUMBER: four
DIRECTION: southeast
BODY PART: hipbone
FAMILY MEMBER: eldest daughter
AREA: to the far left when standing at the door looking inward

Revealing Exercises:

Answers in red suggest conditions favorable to prosperity.

- ❑ yes ❑ no 1. All of the bowls, vases, planters, candleholders, and other objects in my space that were designed with the intention of being filled are filled.
- ❑ yes ❑ no 2. My refrigerator is filled with an abundance of fresh and healthful foods.
- ❑ yes ❑ no 3. In my space, I have represented symbols of abundant, vital life forms: water fountains, fish tanks, plants and flowers, bowls of fresh fruit and vegetables, crystals and other objects from the earth, pets, wind chimes.
- ❑ yes ❑ no 4. I have books, reports, files, clothes, or other objects that I have not used or that have not served me in the last year in my prosperity corners.
- ❑ yes ❑ no 5. I have trashcans in the prosperity area of my space.
- ❑ yes ❑ no 6. I keep my toilet seat down and the door to my bathroom closed when it is not in use.
- ❑ yes ❑ no 7. I have leaky faucets, drains, and pipes in my space.
- ❑ yes ❑ no 8. I have knives, scissors, or other sharp objects in the prosperity corners of my space.
- ❑ yes ❑ no 9. My checkbook is accurately and neatly balanced and I always know how much cash is in my wallet.
- ❑ yes ❑ no 10. All of the prosperity areas in my space are well lit.

Applications

1. Place all checks made out to you in a tray in the prosperity corner of your desk to attract an incoming flow of financial energy. A green or purple wooden tray will strengthen this energy.

2. The stove is the single most important indicator of wealth in your environment. It is associated with both the financial and health energy of the space.

Tips for sustaining and activating this energy:

- *Ensure that you use all four burners equally, thereby improving your cash flow.*
- *Place a mirror or other reflective object behind the stove, to reflect the burners and double your prosperity.*
- *If you do not cook at home, make an effort to turn on oven and burners often to maintain the flow of prosperous energy.*
- *Ensure that your stove is in optimal working order. Clean it thoroughly, and don't neglect the spaces underneath and behind.*

3. To be in control of your life and your finances, you must place yourself within the command position of your space. When facing the entryway, the command position is the area farthest from the door, but not in line with the door. From the command position, you can see everything that goes on in the room, including entrances and departures. The master bedroom and the executive office should occupy the command position of a space. The bed, desk, stove, and sofa should also be placed in this position. If you do not occupy this area, others may control your life or your business. You may feel constantly out of control.

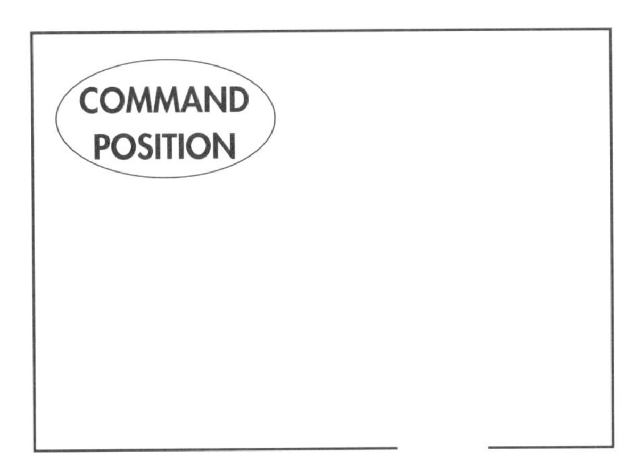

4. Water is an excellent energy source for attracting prosperity, as it serves many purposes. If you need a flow of cash, use moving water in the prosperity area—water fountains, pictures of flowing water, a fish tank with fish in it. If you want to accumulate wealth, work with still water symbols such as lakes, ponds, or swimming pools in the front of your property. Like everything else in our space, these things must be nurtured and cared for. Do not allow the water to become murky or cloudy. Cloudy water represents a less-than-healthy financial picture, whereas clear water symbolizes a calm and clear financial future.

THE WAY I SEE IT, IF YOU WANT THE RAINBOW, YOU GOTTA PUT UP WITH THE RAIN.

DOLLY PARTON

木墨
設計

EVERY MAN IS THE ARCHITECT OF HIS OWN FORTUNE.

SALLUST

FAME

THIS AREA OF OUR LIFE represents how we see ourselves, our state of enlightenment, as well as how we are known in the world.

ELEMENT: fire
CHARACTERISTICS: hot, explosive; consuming and destroying, speeding upward
COLORS: red, purple, pink
SHAPE: angular, flame-like, steeple-like; mountain peak
NUMBER: nine
DIRECTION: south
BODY PART: eyes
FAMILY MEMBER: middle daughter
AREA: When entering a space, this is the far central area.

Revealing Exercises

❑ yes ❑ no 1. My highest diplomas and proudest achievements are prominently displayed in my fame area.

❑ yes ❑ no 2. My name and title are clearly displayed in the fame area of my desk and office.

❑ yes ❑ no 3. All windows and mirrors are clean and free of scratches, chips, and cracks.

❑ yes ❑ no 4. I have a clear view to the front of my home or work environment with no obstructions.

❑ yes ❑ no 5. All windows or doors in this area are partly covered with blinds, curtains, or other design elements to harness and sustain positive fame energy before it can leave my environment.

❑ yes ❑ no 6. I have at least one mirror in each room of my house.

Applications

If you answered "no" to any of the exercises on page 72, you may want to implement the changes recommended below.

1. Since feng shui is about creating balance in our environment, consider the proper placement for major items such as fireplaces and pools. The best place for fire energy—a fireplace, a barbecue—is in the fame area. Should you find water energy here, whether it be pool, pond, or fountain, you will want to create a balance by introducing fire and wood energy—fire because it is the energy associated with this area and wood because wood fuels fire and makes it stronger. By allowing the water to remain here unbalanced, you are diminishing or "putting out" the fire energy.

2. Red is one of the primary colors recommended in the fame area, as it is the most active color. To activate your business, use red lettering on your business cards and stationery. Place your name or your company's name in the top central fame area of the business card.

3. The fame area is connected to the eyes. Since the eyes are the windows to the soul, it is extremely important to ensure that windows and mirrors are kept clear and clean. This guarantees that we have a clear view of our future as well as who we are in the world. Avoid cracks, chips, or splits in windows or mirrors, which distort our view of ourselves and our position in the world.

4. Take a moment in the evening or on a dreary day to walk through your space. Turn the lights on. You may discover that there are corners and even rooms that need new lighting. Allowing these areas to remain dark may lead us to avoid them literally and figuratively. Light allows clarity and vision into our future; it revitalizes stagnant energy. Use full spectrum lighting rather than fluorescent lighting. Full spectrum lightbulbs are closest to natural sunlight and flicker less than fluorescent bulbs. The rapid flickering of fluorescent lightbulbs affects the rhythm of brainwaves and causes fatigue. Full spectrum lightbulbs are available at most hardware stores, and come in the same shapes and sizes as standard lightbulbs. During the season when sunlight is at a minimum, additional lighting may help offset the occurrence of Seasonal Affective Disorder (SAD), caused by a deficiency of natural sunlight.

WHEN YOU GIVE OF YOURSELF, YOU RECEIVE MORE THAN YOU GIVE.

ANTOINE DE SAINT-EXUPÉRY

No external advantages can supply self-reliance. The force of one's being ... must come from within.

R. W. Clark

木墨設計

WHAT WE STEADILY, CONSCIOUSLY, HABITUALLY THINK WE ARE, THAT WE TEND TO BECOME.

ANN LANDERS

CREATIVITY AND CHILDREN

THIS AREA REPRESENTS our creative output in the world—both general creativity and the making of children. It represents happiness and potential.

ELEMENT: metal
CHARACTERISTICS: contracting, heavy, cold, stagnant; inward movement
COLORS: white, pastels
SHAPE: domed, oval, arched
NUMBER: seven
DIRECTION: west
BODY PART: lungs, mouth
FAMILY MEMBER: youngest daughter
AREA: When entering a space, this area is to the right of center.

Revealing Exercises

1. My favorite color is

because it makes me feel

2. My walls are filled with

3. My environment is painted in my favorite colors of

4. The most fun I had recently was

5. The last time I laughed so hard I cried was

6. My desk is positioned so that I face

7. The last time I got an inspiring idea was

Applications

1. Free your soul from inhibitions. Be a child again. If you do not normally spend time with kids, spend an hour, half a day, or even a weekend with a child. Children are the best teachers of creativity. They express themselves freely, as they do not yet know the fear of failure. Follow their lead: use your entire body to move, explore, and expand into your space.

2. Infertility has become a major issue in our society. The physical and emotional challenge can be great. If you would like to conceive a child, place items that represent children—stuffed animals, a rocking chair—in this area. Plant a new seed to represent the baby that may soon be growing in your belly.

3. Environments for creative expression—art studios, writing areas—should be placed in this area to capitalize on the abundant creative energy. In a child's room, you can set up a table or ballet barre here.

4. To increase your children's energy, locate their bedroom in this area of the home. Alternatively, place their beds in the children's area of the room, taking care not to place them directly opposite the door (see diagrams). Place children's beds against the wall to give them the support they need until they become teenagers.

5. Walls and columns block our creativity and vision. If your desk faces a wall, creative energy cannot flow in front of you, and it is more difficult to access from behind. Place desks facing out into the room.

6. If we leave the walls of this area empty, our creative energy will be stagnant. Place inspiring objects here to get the creative juices flowing.

7. Color energy serves many healing purposes. By integrating colors into our creative area, we capitalize on this energy.

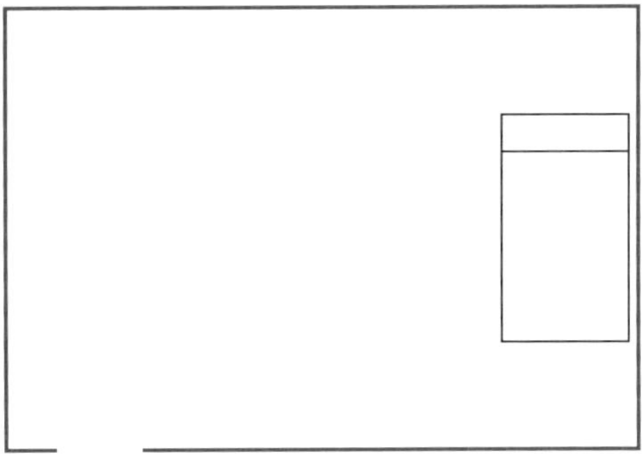

correct bed placement

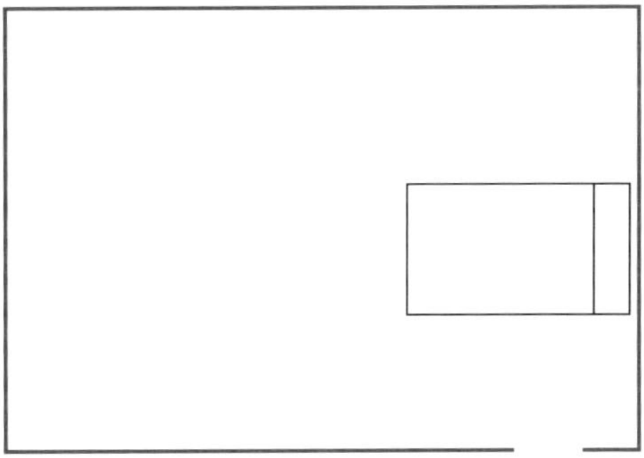

incorrect

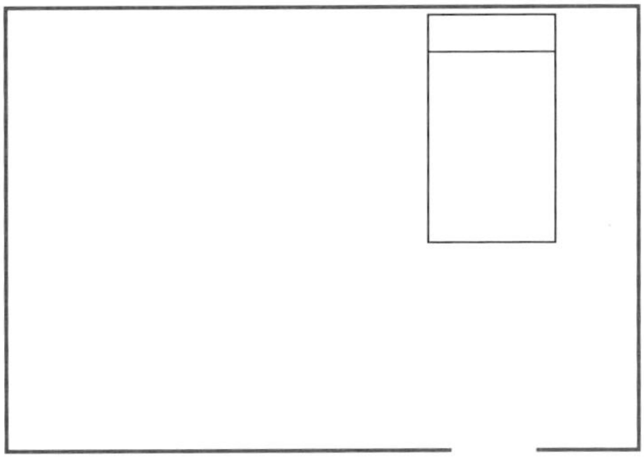

incorrect

木墨設計

木墨
設計

IN THE LONG RUN, MEN HIT ONLY WHAT THEY AIM AT. THEREFORE, THOUGH THEY SHOULD FAIL IMMEDIATELY, THEY HAD BETTER AIM AT SOMETHING HIGH.

HENRY DAVID THOREAU

水墨設計

HELPFUL PEOPLE AND TRAVEL

THIS AREA OF OUR LIFE represents all those who are helpful to us as well as our helpfulness to others. It is also associated with travel: we explore and discover new places and things in order to benefit others and ourselves.

ELEMENT: metal
CHARACTERISTICS: contracting, heavy, cold, stagnant, inward movement
COLORS: gray, black, white, silver, gold, bronze
SHAPE: domed, oval, arched
NUMBER: six
DIRECTION: northwest
BODY PART: head
FAMILY MEMBER: father
AREA: When entering a space, this area is to the near right.

Revealing Exercises

❑ yes ❑ no *1.* Helpful people exist or appear in my life when I need them.

❑ yes ❑ no *2.* I am helpful to others in proportion to their helpfulness to me.

❑ yes ❑ no *3.* As I receive more in my life, I give back more.

❑ yes ❑ no *4.* My degree of helpfulness is commensurate with my prosperity.

❑ yes ❑ no *5.* I would like to travel more than I do now.

❑ yes ❑ no *6.* On a monthly basis, I freely volunteer my time for a good cause and feel rewarded by it.

❑ yes ❑ no *7.* There are at least two people in my life whom I can call at any time of the day or night.

❑ yes ❑ no *8.* I have a good and loving relationship with my father.

❑ yes ❑ no *9.* I have helpful male friends and family members on whom I can rely.

APPLICATIONS

1. Make a list of all the people who have helped you within the last three months. Ask each of them sincerely if there is anything you can do for them. Expect nothing in return.

2. Put a quarter in an expired meter with a car next to it. Someone will do the same for you one day when you need it!

3. Since heavenly energies are also associated with this area, hang a metal wind chime with six angels in your space, and ring it every day between 11:00 and 1:00 to activate and circulate the helpful people energy in your life.

4. Place a globe or map of the next place you would like to visit in the travel area. Use markers to specify the exact route of your trip. Frame the map in a metal frame or place the globe in a metal base to help activate travel energy.

5. This area holds the most male energy. Any heavy objects or blocks in this area can create barriers in our relationships with our fathers or other males in our lives. Clear this area of large and immovable pieces of furniture.

FOLLOW THE WAY OF HEAVEN, REFLECT ON THE PRINCIPLE BEHIND HUMAN AFFAIRS.

HAN FEI TZU, THIRD CENTURY B.C.

木墨設計

木墨
設計

FAMILY AND GROWTH

THIS AREA REPRESENTS family, families of friends and colleagues, ancestors, new growth, and opportunity.

ELEMENT: wood
CHARACTERISTICS: expansive, upward movement; consuming and creating, sprouting
COLORS: green, blue, purple
SHAPE: tall, thin; pillar-like
NUMBER: three
DIRECTION: east
BODY PART: foot
FAMILY MEMBER: eldest son
AREA: When entering a space, this area is to the left of center.

REVEALING EXERCISES

1. The things that my family enjoys doing together on a regular basis are:

2. The last time my family did anything together was when:

3. My employees tend to agree with one another when:

4. The family area of my environment is used for the following purposes:

5. The family area of my environment is full of:

6. The last time I experienced growth and opportunity in my life was when:

7. My grandparents and great-grandparents were born in the town and country of:

8. My grandfather and grandmother worked for a living as:

Applications

1. Ideally, the family or gathering room of your space should be situated in the family and growth area.

2. Refer to your floor plan. If this area is missing, place a large mirror on the wall closest to the missing area to draw the missing energy into your environment.

3. Place three real or silk green plants or trees here to represent new growth potential.

4. Hang pictures of your family and ancestors in the growth area to honor your heritage. Choose photographs of happy times. Use frames made of wood.

5. Place books, games, puzzles, and other interactive materials in this area to encourage family participation.

6. Plan monthly, semi-annual, and annual trips and reunions for the entire family. Stick to your plans.

7. Position the furniture in a way that is conducive to conversation. Don't place single chairs in corners away from the main area of the room.

8. Enclose the television in a cabinet with a door; close the cabinet when the television is off. Keep group viewing to a minimum. Television prevents meaningful conversation and interaction.

木墨
設計

If ye don't know the past, then ye will not have a future. If ye don't know where your people have been, then ye won't know where your people are going.

Forrest Carter

KNOWLEDGE

THIS AREA REPRESENTS knowledge, wisdom, self-cultivation, and spiritual development—the potential to grow from within.

ELEMENT: earth
CHARACTERISTICS: firm but not rigid; stable, reliable; still but not stagnant
COLORS: blue, green, clay, yellow
SHAPE: low, flat, square, plateau
NUMBER: eight
DIRECTION: northeast
BODY PART: hand
FAMILY MEMBER: youngest son
AREA: When entering a space, this area is to the near left.

REVEALING EXERCISES

1. If I could be doing anything in life, I would be:

2. I nurture and cultivate myself by:

3. The last learning experience I had was:

4. The area in my space where I spend quiet time is:

5. In the knowledge area of my space, I have the following objects:

6. In looking at my floor plan, the knowledge area of my first floor falls primarily in the following room(s):

7. I balance my work life and personal life by:

____

____

____

❑ yes ❑ no 8. I am doing what I am most passionate about in life.

❑ yes ❑ no 9. I spend at least three hours a week nurturing and cultivating myself in some way.

❑ yes ❑ no 10. I am open to new experiences without judgment.

❑ yes ❑ no 11. I exercise in some way at least 2 hours a week.

❑ yes ❑ no 12. There is an area in my environment designated solely for quiet time—reading, learning, meditating.

❑ yes ❑ no 13. I am beginning to understand that my actions and reactions have a ripple effect on the community at large.

❑ yes ❑ no 14. The knowledge area of my space is well organized and free of clutter and unused items.

❑ yes ❑ no 15. When I look at my floor plan, this area is missing completely or partially.

Applications:

1. Designate a sacred space in the knowledge area for the purpose of studying, learning, developing intuition, meditating; honoring yourself and your teachers; renewing your spiritual beliefs and principles; and being at peace.

2. Place your desk or your child's desk in the knowledge area to activate energy and increase learning and understanding.

3. Put the library or bookcase in this area.

4. Use four pairs of blue ceramic bookends to help cultivate knowledge energy.

5. Energize all of your senses. Use incense, aromatherapy, color, music, and bells. Integrate eight blue or green candles or plush pillows here to create a calming, peaceful energy.

6. Place a fan or other moving item here to clear the energy.

7. Integrate stable, grounding mountain energy into the knowledge area. A sacred box or other vessel can represent the containing energy of the mountain.

木墨
設計

HEALTH

THIS AREA REPRESENTS our overall health, our sense of being in balance with the universe.

ELEMENT: earth, in transition from seed to harvest
CHARACTERISTICS: firm but not rigid; stable, reliable; still but not stagnant
COLORS: yellow, orange, gold, clay
SHAPE: low, flat, square; plateau
NUMBER: five
DIRECTION: center; no direction
BODY PART: all other body parts
FAMILY MEMBER: seventh child—bringing outside influences to the family
AREA: This area is at the absolute center.

REVEALING EXERCISES

Checklist for good health:

- ☐ *1.* This area is clean, clear, orderly, and clutter-free.
- ☐ *2.* There are no old, unused, or decaying items in the health area anywhere on my property, including sheds, equipment, and cars.
- ☐ *3.* There are no divisions, splits, or bathrooms in this area.
- ☐ *4.* I do not feel tired, drained, or overwhelmed in my environment.
- ☐ *5.* There are no beams or low, slanted ceilings in my environment.
- ☐ *6.* There are no sharp, pointed corners or protruding angles in my environment.

Applications

1. Hang a crystal in the health area or near the closest window. Crystals come from the earth and possess healing qualities. They help to harness the positive energies of nature. When the sun catches a crystal, a beautiful rainbow spectrum of colors appears throughout the space, producing joy and wonderment.

2. Soften any sharp corners or protruding angles by placing a plant directly in front of the point, stenciling along the point, or placing a crystal there to disperse the piercing energy.

3. Create an open, uncluttered area where you can move easily and effortlessly. You should feel balanced and energized.

4. To create balance in the health area, integrate all the elemental energies—wood, fire, metal, water, earth—or all the colors of the bagua.

5. Ensure there are no divisions in the health area such as a wall or staircase. If it cannot be helped, create union by placing a mirror on each side of the wall that separates the space, or unify the staircase by wrapping ivy around the railings.

6. Place in this area symbols of good health—infinity, yin and yang—or scales representing balance in life.

7. Arrange a colorful assortment of fresh flowers here to bring in the healing colors of the rainbow.

8. Display a horn of plenty representing abundant and vital earth energy.

9. Add up-lighting, a crystal, or an uplifting picture—of a hot air balloon, for example—to lift the oppressive energy of overhead beams or slanted ceilings.

木墨設計

木墨
設計

FENG SHUI MEANS "WIND AND WATER." WIND IS THE ENERGY OF OUR BREATH; WATER REPRESENTS HOW WE CHOOSE TO EXIST IN THE FLOW OF OUR LIFE.